NOTE TO PARENTS

Welcome to Kingfisher Readers! This program is designed to help young readers build skills, confidence, and a love of reading as they explore their favorite topics.

These tips can help you get more from the experience of reading books together. But remember, the most important thing is to make reading fun!

Tips to Warm Up Before Reading

- Look through the book with your child. Ask them what they notice about the pictures.
- Wonder aloud together. Ask questions and make predictions. What will this book be about? What are some words we could expect to find on these pages?

While Reading

- Take turns or read together until your child takes over.
- Point to the words as you say them.
- When your child gets stuck on a word, ask if the picture could help. Then think about the first letter too.
- Accept and praise your child's contributions.

After Reading

- Look back at the things your child found interesting. Encourage connections to other things you both know.
- Draw pictures or make models to explore these ideas.
- Read the book again soon, to build fluency.

With five distinct levels and a wealth of appealing topics, the Kingfisher Readers series provides children with an exciting way to learn to read about the world around them. Enjoy!

Ellie Costa, M.S. Ed.
Literacy Specialist, Bank Street School for Children, New York

KINGFISHER
READERS

level
3

Robots

Chris Oxlade

KINGFISHER
NEW YORK

KINGFISHER
LONDON & NEW YORK
Copyright © Kingfisher 2017
Published in the United States by Kingfisher,
175 Fifth Ave., New York, NY 10010
Kingfisher is an imprint of Pan Macmillan, London.
All rights reserved.

Distributed in the U.S. and Canada by Macmillan,
175 Fifth Ave., New York, NY 10010

Library of Congress Cataloging-in-Publication Data

Names: Oxlade, Chris, author.
Title: Robots / Chris Oxlade.
Description: New York, NY : Kingfisher, 2017. | Series: Kingfisher readers |
   Audience: Age 6. | Audience: K to grade 3.
Identifiers: LCCN 2016049242| ISBN 9780753473436 (hardback) | ISBN
   9780753473443 (paperback)
Subjects: LCSH: Robots--Juvenile literature. | BISAC: JUVENILE NONFICTION /
   Technology / Inventions. | JUVENILE NONFICTION / Readers / Beginner. |
   JUVENILE NONFICTION / Technology / Electricity & Electronics.
Classification: LCC TJ211.2 .O87 2017 | DDC 629.8/92--dc23
LC record available at https://lccn.loc.gov/2016049242

Series editor: Thea Feldman
Literacy consultant: Ellie Costa, Bank Street College, New York
Design: Peter Clayman

978-0-7534-7343-6 (HB)
978-0-7534-7344-3 (PB)

Kingfisher books are available for special promotions
and premiums. For details contact: Special Markets
Department, Macmillan, 175 Fifth Ave., New York, NY 10010.

For more information, please visit
www.kingfisherbooks.com

Printed in China

9 8 7 6 5 4 3 2 1

1TR/0317/WKT/UG/105MA

Picture credits
The Publisher would like to thank the following for permission to reproduce their material.
Top = t; Bottom = b; Center = c; Left = l; Right = r
Cover NASA; Pages 4 Shutterstock/Photodiem; 5 Getty/Syfy/Contributor; 6l Wikipedia/Creative
Commons; 7 Getty/Science & Society Picture Library/Contributor; 8 Getty/ERIC PIERMONT/
Staff; 9t iStock/Jaroslav Frank, 9b Alamy/Macrocosmos; 10 ABB/new.abb.com; 11 iStock/Alexey
Dudoladov; 12 Getty/Junko Kimura/Staff; 13 Getty/Chesnot/Contributor; 14 NASA; 15 Alamy/ MixPix;
16 iStock/RuslanDashinsky; 17t Shutterstock/avarand, 17b Shutterstock/Thatsaphons; 18 NASA;
19 Getty/Yamaguchi Haruyoshi/Contributor, 20 Getty/Justin Sullivan/Staff; 22–23 Alamy/Xinhua; 24
Shutterstock/Tinxi; 25 iStock; 26 Alamy/age fotostock, 27t Alamy/615 collection, 27b Alamy/WENN
Ltd; 28 Getty/Silver Screen Collection, 29 Getty/Kevin Winter.

Contents

What is a robot?

A robot is a machine that can move and do things without the help of a person. Inside each robot is a computer that acts like the robot's brain. A **program** in the computer decides how and when the robot moves.

NAO Evolution robot

Robot wars!
Some robots are built to do battle with each other.

obots come in a wide variety of shapes and
izes, and do many different jobs. They work
n factories, in homes, at theme parks, high
n the air, and even deep under the sea!

Before robots

About 500 years ago, before there were the kinds of robots we have today, there were simpler machines called **automatons**. Automatons could play musical instruments, write letters, and dance. In 1738, a French inventor built a duck that flapped its wings, ate food, and even quacked!

Very creative! This automaton, built by inventor Henri Maillardet in 1800, could write and draw pictures!

UNI

In 1920, a Czech writer named Karel Capek invented the word "robot" when he was writing a play. The word comes from the Czech word *robota*, which means "hard work."

The first robot that was used in a factory was called Unimate. Beginning in 1961, it helped to build cars.

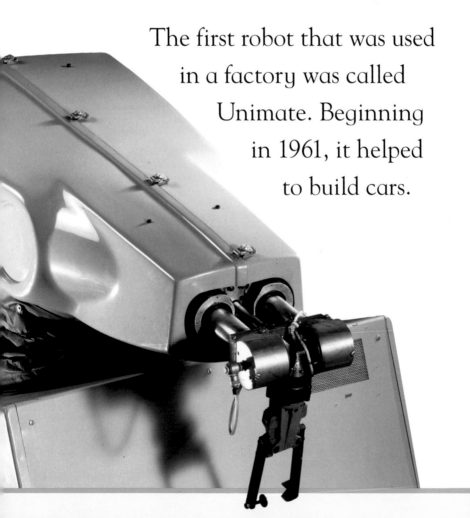

Robots at home

Today, there are robots that work in people's homes! There are robots that can **automatically** clean carpets, sweep floors, wash windows, or cut grass.

Best Buddy!
Helper robots, such as this one called Buddy, can find information on the Internet and play games with children.

The little robot next to the dog works like a vacuum cleaner. It moves across

the floor, sucking up dust as it goes. When it reaches a wall or a piece of furniture, it automatically turns round.

There is no one robot that can do every household job yet, but there might be someday!

lawn-mowing robot

Factory robots

Most robots work in factories. They lift and move heavy objects. They use tools to cut, drill, and shape **materials**, and to tighten screws, nuts, and bolts. Factory robots can also be called industrial robots.

YuMi robot

Lend a hand!
The YuMi robot is a small robot that can work side by side with people in factories.

The robots in the photo below are built like human arms. Each has joints that move, and the end of each arm can hold different tools in the same way that a human hand can. This can include a tool to pick up objects, a screwdriver to tighten screws, or a spray gun to spray paint.

Sensing and moving

Your five senses—touch, sight, hearing, taste, and smell—tell you all about the world around you. Robots have and use senses too. A robot might have touch **sensors** that tell it when it has bumped into something. Another robot might have a video camera so it can see what is around it.

On the move!

Electric motors make a robot move. The robot's computer switches its motors on and off.

Many robots move along on wheels or tracks. Others walk on legs. Some robots have two legs, some have four legs, and some have as many as six or eight legs!

Robots as explorers

A space **probe** explores other planets
and moons. Some probes land on the
surface of a moon or planet to take a closer
look, and some, called rovers, even drive
around to explore! Humans back on Earth
operate space probes.

NASA's *Curiosity*
rover has been on
Mars since 2012.

Underwater robots

An underwater robot that is steered by remote control, like the one in this picture, is called a remotely operated vehicle, or ROV.

Robots also work in the deep sea! They send back photographs and videos of the ocean floor, marine animals, and even shipwrecks. They can help to fix oil pipes and underwater cables too.

Drones

A drone is a flying robot that works as an "eye in the sky." It has an on-board video camera that records images, or sends them to a screen on a handset, tablet, or computer.

rotor

Lifting up!
Drones have spinning **rotors** that lift them into the air. Smaller, lighter drones have four or more rotors, but larger, heavier drones have six or even eight rotors.

Drones can film soccer games, bicycle races, or concerts. Some people use them to film themselves and their friends while they are mountain biking, skateboarding, or snowboarding.

A person uses a **remote control** to fly a drone. A drone can be made to fly up, down, forward, and backward. Some drones can fly themselves and are programmed to return to their starting point.

remote control

Robots that look like us

Scientists and engineers build robots that look like humans, move like humans, and even behave like humans!

A **humanoid** robot is a robot that has the same body shape as a human. It has a **torso**, a head, and two arms, but it still looks like a machine. Some humanoids move on wheels and some walk on legs.

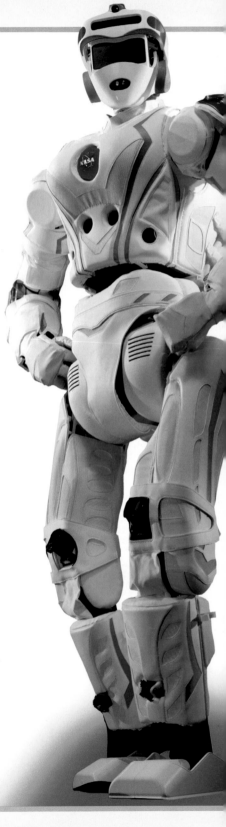

Androids look exactly like humans! An android has lifelike skin and a face that can smile or frown. Androids can also talk, and some can answer simple questions. One day, it may be hard to tell humans and androids apart!

Otonaroid, a Japanese android

Robots to the rescue

Some robots do jobs that would be too dangerous for humans. Robots are sent to examine bags, cars, or trucks that might contain hidden bombs. An expert operates the robot with a remote control. The robot carries tools that will destroy a bomb.

bomb-disposal robot

Firefighting robots help firefighters put out flames. The robots go into places that would be too hot or smoky for humans to go. Firefighters also fly drones above burning buildings, using an **infrared camera** to find the hottest parts of a fire.

Robots play sports and games

Some robots play soccer, chess, and other games. Scientists and engineers also build robots to test how well they will do with sports. The scientists want to see how smart the robots can be.

The RoboCup is a soccer match for robots. The robots play in teams, pass the ball to each other, and try to score goals. They can't beat human soccer players, but they are getting better each year!

Robot toys

Toymakers began to make toy robots nearly 100 years ago. Today there are toy humanoid robots, robot vehicles, robot pets and monsters, talking robots, and robots from sci-fi films.

Learning is fun!
Robot toys are a great way to learn about science, technology, engineering, and math.

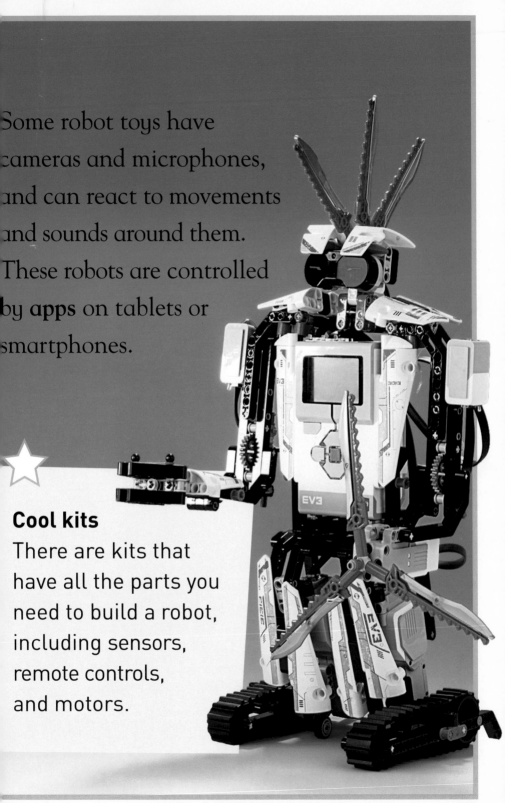

Some robot toys have cameras and microphones, and can react to movements and sounds around them. These robots are controlled by **apps** on tablets or smartphones.

Cool kits
There are kits that have all the parts you need to build a robot, including sensors, remote controls, and motors.

Robots in battle

Military robots help armies and air
forces on the battlefield and in the air.
They spy on enemy forces, which would
be too dangerous for soldiers and pilots.

camera

Military drones are also called unmanned
aerial vehicles, or UAVs. They take photos
and film as they fly. Some even carry
missiles to fire.

A small, spy robot can travel across rough ground on tracks. It is operated by a soldier with a remote control. The robot sends pictures of enemy positions back to the soldier.

Big Dog!
This robot, called Big Dog, was built to carry a heavy load across a bumpy battlefield.

Robots in the movies

Many sci-fi and fantasy movies now include specially created robots. Movie robots can be frightening or friendly, miniature or giant, and can have incredible powers! Moviemakers begin by making detailed models of the robots or by creating robots with computer-generated imagery, or CGI.

Robots have been appearing in movies for a long time. A giant alien robot called Gort stepped out of a flying saucer in a 1951 film called *The Day the Earth Stood Still.*

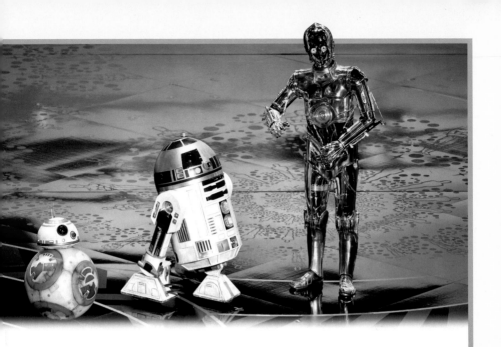

Perhaps the three most famous movie robots are BB8, R2-D2 and C-3PO from *Star Wars*. C-3PO is a gold-colored humanoid robot programmed to always be polite to humans.

Giant Gort
Gort was played by an actor who was 7.5 feet (2.3 meters) tall and wore a foam suit!

Glossary

android a robot that looks exactly like a human

app a set of instructions on a smartphone or tablet

automatically working without help

automaton a mechanical human or animal, like a robot, with parts that move

CGI computer-generated imagery, which means images that are drawn by computer

humanoid a robot that looks like a human

infrared camera a camera that can see heat and find the hottest parts of a burning building

marine from the sea

materials things that are used to make other objects

missile a weapon that is fired to hit faraway places

program instructions put into a computer that tell a robot what to do

remote control a tool that allows a person to operate a robot from a distance

motor the part of a machine that turns

sensor a tool, such as a video camera, that helps a robot find out about its surroundings

Index

If you have enjoyed reading this book, look
out for more in the Kingfisher Readers series!

KINGFISHER READERS: LEVEL 3

☐ Ancient Rome
☐ Astronauts
☐ Cars
☐ Creepy Crawlies
☐ Dinosaur World
☐ Firefighters
☐ Record Breakers—The Biggest
☐ Robots
☐ Vikings
☐ Volcanoes

Collect
and read
them all!

KINGFISHER READERS: LEVEL 4

☐ The Arctic and Antarctica
☐ Flight
☐ Human Body
☐ Pirates
☐ Rivers
☐ Sharks
☐ Spiders
☐ Weather

For a full list of Kingfisher Readers books, plus guidance for
teachers and parents and activities and fun stuff for kids, go to
the Kingfisher Readers website: www.kingfisherreaders.com